The Nature Kid's Guide to

SHEEP

Level 2

DAVID ANDERSON

LP Media Inc. Publishing

For information address LP Media Inc. Publishing,
30012 Variolite St NW, Princeton MN 55371
www.lpmedia.org

Publication Data

Sheep
The Nature Kid's Guide to Sheep — First edition.

Summary: "Learn all about Sheep, the Nature Kid Way"
— Provided by publisher.

ISBN: 979-8-89818-177-2

[1. Sheep – Non-Fiction] I. Title.

Title: The Nature Kid's Guide to Sheep

CONTENTS

SHEEP SHACKS

There are more than one billion sheep living on Earth right now!

Baa! A fluffy sheep trots out of its cozy red barn.

Sheep live on farms all over the world, from the green hills of New Zealand to the rocky highlands of Scotland. Some graze on wide open plains, while others roam steep mountain pastures high above the clouds.

It was not always this way. Thousands of years ago, all sheep were wild. Then people began taming them for their wool, milk, and meat.

Today, some sheep sleep in cozy barns with soft straw on the floor. Others live out on open rangeland with only a shepherd and a trusty dog to watch over them.

WILD WOOLIES

Wild sheep called mouflons still live in parts of Europe and Asia!

Clack! A Scottish Blackface ram leaps from rock to rock on a steep hill.

The wild relatives of today's sheep lived in the rocky mountains of Asia. They were fast and tough, with thin, rough coats that were not fluffy at all.

Over time, farmers picked the wooliest sheep to keep. Little by little, sheep grew thicker, softer coats. The rough, scratchy hair became the warm, fluffy **fleece** we know today.

Some breeds are still tough like their wild ancestors. Scottish Blackface sheep have strong legs, dark faces, and wiry wool made for cold, windy mountains.

SIZE UP

Stomp! A big ram stares down a sheepdog that is trying to herd it.

Stand next to a sheep and you might be surprised. Most sheep come up to about your waist, but they are much heavier than they look. All that fluffy wool hides a strong, thick body underneath!

The biggest sheep are really heavy. A Suffolk ram can weigh over 250 pounds, more than most grown-ups! But all that weight is hidden under a big poofy coat of soft wool.

Not all sheep are huge. Some breeds like the Shetland are small enough for a kid to hug. Big or small, every sheep has strong legs made for climbing hills and running fast.

FLUFFY FEATURES

Whoosh! A Valais blacknose sheep grazes with his herd.

Sheep have round bodies covered in wool. Their legs are thin but strong. Two small ears stick out from the sides of their head.

Most sheep have split hooves on each foot. These hooves help them walk on bumpy ground. Some sheep also have curly horns.

Valais Blacknose sheep look extra special. They have fuzzy black faces and floppy ears. Their fluffy wool hangs down like a big blanket.

Sheep have no top front teeth, just hard gums that help them chew grass!

SUPER SENSES

Sniff! A Jacob sheep lifts its nose and smells a friend nearby.

Sheep have great senses that help keep them safe. Their eyes sit on the sides of their head. This lets them see almost all the way around!

Their ears can twist and turn to catch sounds. They hear soft noises from far away. This helps them know when danger is close.

With eyes that see nearly everything and ears that miss almost nothing, sneaking up on a sheep is harder than you think!

Sheep have special pupils shaped like rectangles, not circles!

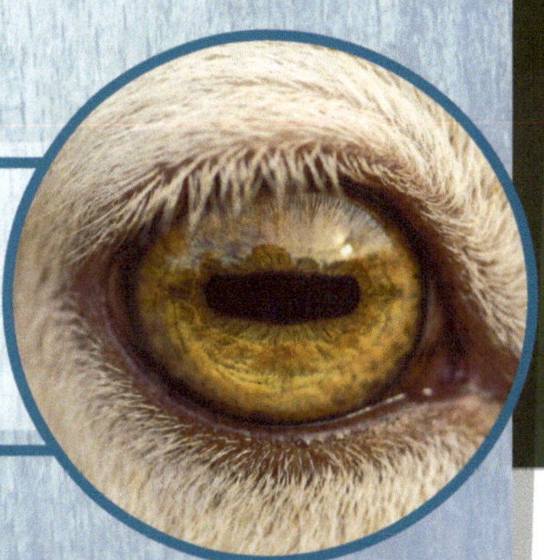

SO MANY SHEEP

Click! A farmer counts his herd of Corriedale sheep as they walk through the gate.

Sheep come in many shapes and colors. Some are white, and some are brown or black. A few even have spots or patches!

Each kind of sheep is called a **breed**. Some breeds have long, curly wool. Others have short, smooth hair.

Corriedale sheep are one of the most popular breeds in the world. They were first bred in New Zealand by mixing two other breeds together. Their thick, soft wool is perfect for making cozy sweaters and warm blankets.

GRASS GRAZERS

Munch! A sheep rips up a mouthful of fresh green grass.

Sheep eat plants all day long. They love leafy weeds and clover even more than grass. A sheep will munch on almost anything green it can find!

After they swallow, sheep bring the food back up to chew it again. This is called chewing their **cud**. It helps them get more out of every bite.

Scottish Blackface sheep eat tough plants on rocky hills where other animals would go hungry. No matter the breed, all sheep need plenty of fresh water every day.

A sheep has four parts in its stomach to break down tough food!

WONDERFUL WOOL
FUN FACT!
One pound of wool can be spun into a yarn strand over 20 miles long!
18

Buzz! The clippers glide through a thick coat of fluffy wool.

Wool is one of the best things sheep give us. It keeps us warm in winter, cool in summer, and dry in the rain. That is why wool is used to make sweaters, hats, socks, and cozy blankets.

Once a year, farmers shear the wool off using special clippers. It does not hurt at all, just like getting a haircut! Afterward, the sheep feels light and cool, and the wool starts growing right back.

Merino sheep grow the softest wool of any breed. Their thick, fine fleece can weigh ten pounds or more. That is enough wool from just one sheep to make several sweaters!

BAA BAA

DID YOU KNOW?
Sheep can remember the faces of up to 50 other sheep for years!

Baaaa! A lamb cries out and its mother calls right back.

Sheep talk to each other by making sounds. The most common sound is "baa," but every sheep has its own voice.

A loud, sharp baa can mean danger is close. Soft, low sounds mean a sheep feels safe and happy. Lambs cry out for their mothers when they wander too far away.

Sheep also talk with their bodies. A stomp of the foot means "I am scared!" and a head butt means "move over!" Once you know what to look for, sheep have a lot to say.

SHEEP
SCHEDULE
22

Rustle! A Dorper ram pushes through the gate at sunrise.

Sheep like a set routine each day. They wake up early and start eating right away. Most of the morning is spent munching on grass.

In the afternoon, sheep rest and chew their cud. They lie down in the shade when it is hot. This quiet time helps them save energy.

Dorper sheep live in warm places. They rest more during the hottest part of the day. When the sun goes down, they eat again.

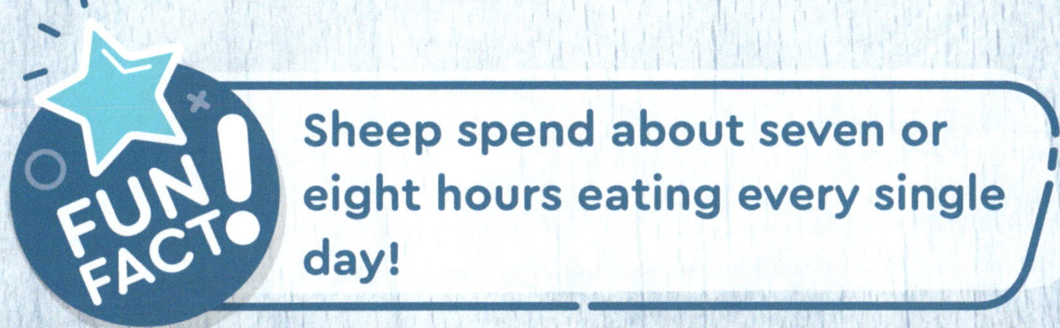

CLIMB HIGH

Sheep can run about 20 miles per hour when they need to escape!
DID YOU KNOW?
24

Scramble! A Scottish Blackface sheep climbs a steep hillside like it is nothing.

Sheep may look slow, but they can move fast. When scared, they run together as a group. This helps keep them safe from danger.

Their strong legs carry them over hills and fields. Sheep are good at climbing steep paths. They can even jump over low fences!

Scottish Blackface sheep are great climbers. They scramble up steep, high slopes with ease. These tough sheep can handle any rough ground.

SILLY SHEEP

Boing! A playful lamb bounces and hops across the meadow.

Sheep do many funny things each day. Lambs love to play and jump around. They bounce on all four legs at once — it looks so silly!

Some sheep rub their backs on fence posts. Others tilt their heads and stare at things. Sheep can be very curious animals.

Valais Blacknose sheep are extra playful. Their shaggy coats bounce as they run. People love to watch them hop and play.

Sheep wag their tails when they are happy, just like dogs do!

FLOCK FRIENDS
FUN FACT!
Sheep make best friends and like to stand close to their buddy!

Patter! A sheep runs to catch up with the rest of the flock.

Sheep love to be with other sheep. A group of sheep is called a **flock**. Most flocks have between 20 and 100 sheep.

Sheep feel safe in a flock. If one sheep gets left behind, it gets upset and cries out until it finds the group again. They do not like being alone at all!

Here is the cool part. Sheep take turns leading the flock! One sheep will lead for a while, then another takes over. Scientists found that by sharing the job, the whole flock gets smarter about finding food and staying safe.

RAM BATTLES

FUN
FACT!
A ewe carries her babies for about
five months before they are born!

Bump! Two big rams push and shove to show who is the strongest.

A male sheep is called a ram. A female sheep is called a **ewe**. In fall, rams try to win the ewes by showing off.

Rams push and bump heads to prove they are tough. The strongest ram becomes the dominant male, but a female sheep leads the flock. After mating, the ewe will have babies in spring.

Suffolk ewes often have twin lambs. Some even have triplets! Most lambs are born between March and May.

LITTLE LAMBS

Bleat! A tiny lamb wobbles, it's still finding its feet!

Lambs are born with soft, curly coats and wobbly legs. But they do not stay wobbly for long. Most lambs can stand up and walk just minutes after being born!

For the first few weeks, lambs drink their mother's milk. Soon they start nibbling on grass and clover too. They grow fast and love to race and jump around the field.

Valais Blacknose lambs might be the cutest of all. With their fuzzy black faces and fluffy white wool, they look like little stuffed animals come to life!

MAMA
KNOWS

Huff! A mother sheep breathes warm air onto her tiny new lamb.

Mother sheep, called ewes, take great care of their lambs. Right after birth, a ewe licks her baby clean. This helps them bond right away.

A ewe knows her own lamb by its smell. She will not feed another ewe's baby. She stays close and guards her lamb from danger.

Merino ewes are caring mothers. They call to their lambs with soft sounds. The pair stays side by side for many weeks.

Twin lambs almost always stay best friends for their whole lives!

HARD
WORKERS

Crunch! A sheep chomps on thick weeds growing in a farmer's yard.

Sheep help people in many ways. Their wool makes warm clothes. Their milk can be used to make cheese. The oil in their wool is used to make lip balm and lotion!

Some sheep help by eating weeds. They mow fields and yards just by grazing! This saves farmers a lot of work.

Sheep even help keep people safe. In some places, flocks graze on dry brush and tall grass to help prevent wildfires.

Sheep can learn their own name and will come when a farmer calls!

BEST
BUDDIES

Clip-clop! A sheep walks side by side with its goat friend.

Sheep get along with just about every animal on the farm. They share fields with goats, cows, and even chickens. Sheep are gentle and calm, which makes them easy to be around.

Some sheep become best pals with donkeys. Donkeys help guard the flock from coyotes and wolves, and the sheep stick close to their big protector. Sheepdogs also help keep the flock safe, and most sheep learn to trust them.

Llamas and alpacas are sometimes kept with sheep to protect them!

GLOSSARY

breed
A specific type of sheep with its own size, color, and wool.

cud
Food that a sheep brings back up from its stomach to chew again.

ewe
An adult female sheep, often the mother of lambs.

fleece
The thick coat of wool that covers a sheep's body.

flock
A group of sheep that live, eat, and move together.